Healing with Crystals

Discover how to use the energy of crystals to attract good fortune, reduce stress and benefit your mind, body and spirit

LINDSEY JAMES

ISBN-10: 1503120368
ISBN-13: 978-1503120365

CONTENTS

INTRODUCTION

Throughout the chronicles of history, crystals have been prized for their healing properties. Even in our modern era, where every single thing has to be fact driven and provable by science, the number of people who believe in the art of crystal therapy and the fact that it is bettering their lives increases daily.

The healing properties of crystals can be utilized in several different ways. For example, they can be carried, worn, placed on or near your body, and one can even make a healing elixir out of them.

Crystals and other minerals form naturally, making them easy to obtain and with only a little knowledge of the craft, crystal healing can be used by anyone.

A BRIEF HISTORY OF CRYSTAL HEALING

Ancient cultures from all over the world believed that crystals bestow special properties, ranging from overall health to personal protection. Gemstones are referenced in the religious texts of differing civilizations around the world.

Gurus and mystics have long believed that all living things have a life energy or life force. Various cultures have different names for this life force. In Chinese culture life force is known as 'chi,' a term that most of us would be familiar with. Other cultures have different names such as Hawaiian (mana), Hindu (prana), and Hebrew (ruah).

The word crystal derives from ancient Greek, meaning both ice and rock crystal. The ancient Greeks believed that crystals were deep frozen ice and that the crystals had protective/healing properties.

The earliest recorded instance where crystals were used, was in magic formulas created by the Sumerians, an ancient civilization in southern Mesopotamia (now currently the region containing Iraq, Kuwait, Turkey, Iran and parts of Syria).

As an example, hematite, an iron ore, was associated with Ares, the Greek god of war, and soldiers would rub it on their bodies to aid them in battle. As another example, an amulet made from amethyst was believed to protect the wearer from becoming drunk.

The ancient Egyptians used topaz stones for protection against evil spirits, and jade was prized as a healing stone in both China and South America. In Burma rubies were inserted into people's bodies as it was believed to make the wearer invulnerable.

HOW TO USE CRYSTALS

Crystals can be used in a variety of different ways. How you use a crystal will depend on your intended purpose and the properties of the particular crystal. Crystals can be used both actively and passively.

Holding a crystal in your hand when meditating and the 'laying on of stones' are examples of active use, whereas wearing crystal jewelry or placing crystals around your home are examples of passive use.

Crystals are believed to absorb energies from exposure to anyone who has handled them, so when new crystals come into your possession they should be cleansed to remove these energies and then re-energized.

It is important that you use the appropriate cleansing and energizing methods to avoid damaging your crystals. Some crystals dissolve in water, others are damaged by salt, and some may fade if exposed to sunlight for example.

Crystals should also be cleansed and energized regularly and before and after use.

HOW TO CLEANSE CRYSTALS

Different cleansing methods should be used depending on the physical properties of the crystal. Salt and salt water should only be used once and then discarded as these will have absorbed negative energies.

. Some cleansing methods include:

1. Placing crystals in a suitable container and covering them with sea salt for several hours, then rinsing them thoroughly with fresh water.

2. Soaking crystals in sea water (if sea water is not available, soak in a solution of clean water and sea salt) for up to 24 hours then rinse thoroughly with fresh water.

3. Smudging the crystals by holding them in the smoke produced by burning incense for 30 seconds.

HOW TO ENERGIZE CRYSTALS

There are a few common ways to energize crystals, two of the simplest methods are: Washing crystals in running fresh water for 10 to 30 minutes (either in a bowl under a running tap or a mesh bag in a river or stream), and exposing the crystals to sun or moon light for 1 to 2 days.

The following are some methods for using crystals:

WEARING AND CARRYING CRYSTALS

The purpose of wearing or carrying a crystal is to keep it close to your body. This allows the crystal to aid you with your desired outcome. Crystals can be worn in the form of jewelry such as rings, earrings, pendants or necklaces. They can also simply be carried in a pocket. For maximum effect, crystals should be in contact with as much as your skin as possible. Tumble stones are crystals that have been smoothened by tumbling and resemble smooth pebbles. They are a convenient alternative to crystal jewelry as they can be comfortably carried in a pocket.

BIRTHSTONES

Wearing or carrying your 'birthstone', a stone that corresponds with the month of your birth is believed to bring health benefits.

Month	U.S.	U.K	Hindu
January	garnet	garnet	serpent stone
February	amethyst	amethyst	moonstone
March	aquamarine, bloodstone	aquamarine, bloodstone	gold
April	diamond	diamond, rock crystal	diamond
May	emerald	emerald, chrysoprase	emerald
June	pearl, moonstone, alexandrite	pearl, moonstone	pearl
July	ruby	ruby, carnelian	sapphire

Month	U.S.	U.K	Hindu
August	peridot	peridot, sardonyx	ruby
September	sapphire	sapphire, lapis lazuli	zircon
October	opal, tourmaline	opal	coral
November	topaz, citrine	topaz, citrine	cat's-eye
December	turquoise, zircon, tanzanite	tanzanite, turquoise	topaz

CRYSTALS IN YOUR HOME AND WORKPLACE

Crystals can be placed in your home, in your car, or place of work to create a desired atmosphere and even provide protection. Protective crystals, such as turquoise, can be placed outside your home. Rose quartz can placed in a family room to create a loving and harmonious atmosphere.

A stress relieving crystal, such as amethyst, may be beneficial in your place of work. Crystals that have been shaped and polished into spheres and pyramids are not only aesthetically pleasing but also provide all the benefits as well.

MEDITATING WITH CRYSTALS

Another common active crystal use is in mediation. Holding the right crystals in one or both hands when meditating can help to focus your thoughts and energy.

Meditation can be done informally while sitting comfortably in a chair. It is best to meditate somewhere quiet so you can concentrate without interruption. Successful mediation requires you to completely relax and clear all worries and distractions from your mind.

To get ready for meditation, sit in a comfortable position, deliberately relax your muscles, let your breathing slip into a constant rhythm and clear all thoughts from your mind.

At first you might have difficulty keeping your mind clear. As you are not physically engaged in any activity, your mind might wander. Should this happen, make a deliberate effort to clear your thoughts and continue your meditation.

It is not necessary to meditate for any specified period of time. In the beginning, you might find it challenging to meditate longer than a few minutes. However, with practice you should be able to meditate for longer periods.

Meditation is about observing thought instead of reacting to thought. It involves being completely aware of the moment. A meditative state makes you conscious of the truth of who you are which transcends your body and mind. A crystal that would help in mediation is clear quartz.

CRYSTAL AFFIRMATIONS

Crystals can also help when making affirmations. An affirmation is simply a declaration or thought that is intended to create a desired result. When making affirmations pay careful attention to the words that you choose; avoid ambiguous words. This way there isn't any room for interpretation.

It is important when making affirmations that you visualize the outcome as it has already been achieved and imagine how the outcome makes you feel. Pay careful attention to the type of crystal being used because they can impact the outcome of your affirmation.

An affirmation does not have to be complicated or follow a particular form of words, it is simply a declaration you make to achieve a desired outcome.

Express the affirmation as if the desired outcome has already been achieved, for example:

I am working in my dream job

I am living in the home of my dreams

I am happy and healthy

CRYSTAL GRIDS

Using a crystal grid can, at times, can be more powerful than using a single crystal. A crystal grid is the placement of crystals in a geometric pattern to direct energy towards a certain goal. Once laid out in a grid the crystals are charged by your energy and purpose.

Smaller grids can be used to obtain help from your crystals to achieve a desired outcome. Larger grids can be used to surround objects. For example, you could construct a grid around your home or even the perimeter of your property to protect against negative energy.

Crystal grids can be made to be permanent by laying them out in a place where they will not be disturbed. They can even be made movable by constructing them on a tray.

Before laying out, the space for the grids must be cleansed. Ways to do this include: placing bowls of salt or a cluster of crystals in the grid location or the burning of herbs. Once the space has been cleansed the crystals grid can be formed with energized crystals.

To energize crystals for the grid, they need to be held in your hands while the grid pattern is visualized before they are laid out. Different grid patterns are used for different purposes. Some patterns may promote a more grounded environment while others are used for purposes such as healing or increased energy.

Some people choose only to use quartz crystals, while

others assemble sets of different crystals that are complimentary to each other.

Crystal grids are used in much the same way as single crystals are used for affirmations. Once again it is imperative for you to focus on the grid and visualize your outcome or goal as if it has already been achieved.

The following diagram shows the Star of Solomon grid. This is based on the six pointed Star of David and sometimes called the Star of David grid.

This is a popular all-purpose grid and has many uses including affirmations and absent healing.

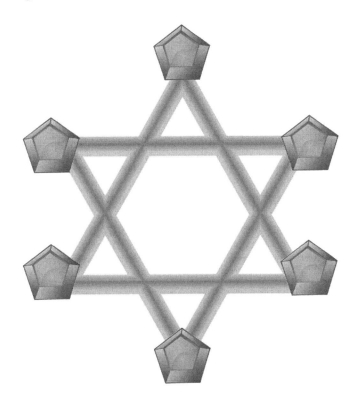

CRYSTALS AND THE CHAKRAS

We all possess an energy field, known as an aura, which both fills and surrounds our bodies. This is connected to the universal energy field by spinning wheels of energy known as Chakras.

Physical illnesses are often the result of psychological challenges. Our mental, emotional and physical health must all be in perfect balance in order for our bodies to function at their best. Our Chakras work to preserve that balance.

Between the base of your spine and top of your head there are seven major Chakras. A blockage in any of your Chakras can cause you to suffer from physical or psychological ailments.

7. Crown Chakra
6. Third eye Chakra

5. Throat Chakra

4. Heart Chakra

3. Solar plexus Chakra

2. Navel Chakra

1. Root Chakra

ROOT CHAKRA

The first Chakra is the root Chakra which enables you to feel safe, grounded and responsible. If it becomes imbalanced, you might feel insecure or anxious. On a physical level, your legs, sexual organs or hips may be affected. Symptoms include muscle cramps, pain in the legs and feet, decreased libido, and lower back pain.

NAVEL CHAKRA

The second Chakra is the navel Chakra which governs confidence and the ability to engage in relationships and relate to other people. If your navel Chakra is out of balance you may become fearful, apathetic, and distrusting of others. You may also struggle to form long term relationships, become sexually absorbed or manipulative.

Physically the navel Chakra is responsible for large intestines, sex organs, bladder and kidneys. Symptoms of Chakra imbalance include constant urination, lower back pain, impotence, cysts and infertility.

SOLAR PLEXUS CHAKRA

The third Chakra is the solar plexus Chakra. This Chakra works to maintain health in your gallbladder, pancreas, small intestine and liver. It also controls impulse, anger, passions and ego.

Rash or irate behavior, addiction and emotional instability

are signs that your solar plexus Chakra is blocked or out of balance. Physical symptoms include indigestion, intestinal problems, liver disorders, food allergies and diabetes.

HEART CHAKRA

The fourth Chakra is the heart Chakra which both physically and metaphorically is responsible for your heart as well as your lungs, upper back and circulation. It affects heart function as well as any love in your life. Psychologically the fourth Chakra connects your body, spirit and mind.

Inadequate coping skills, schizophrenia, phobias, unfaithfulness and neuroses are signs that the fourth Chakra is not balanced... Other symptoms include heart problems, asthma, insomnia, back pain, pain in the upper arm, sore shoulders, some cancers and high blood pressure.

THROAT CHAKRA

The fifth Chakra is the throat Chakra, responsible for your mouth, ears, throat and thyroid. On a psychological level you may become unable to express emotions, anger in particular.

Other mental symptoms include decreased confidence, depression, confusion, insecurity and shyness. Bodily you might become inflicted with ear infections, gum disease, sore throat, hyperthyroidism and other ailments.

THIRD EYE CHAKRA

The sixth Chakra is the third eye Chakra which controls intuition or your ability to see beyond the obvious. It is responsible for your face, brain and eyes. Mental symptoms of a blocked or out of balance sixth Chakra include negativity towards others and selfishness. Physical symptoms include migraines, jaw pain, blurred vision, glaucoma and cancer.

CROWN CHAKRA

The seventh Chakra is the Crown Chakra. This Chakra provides insight and wisdom. It is because of the seventh Chakra that you are aware of the world and your place in it.

If your crown Chakra becomes imbalanced you may feel neurotic, fearful, frustrated, or even psychotic. Your general well-being can be affected and you might feel extremely sad or lost and depressed.

LAYING ON OF STONES

Knowing how to maintain balance within your Chakras and how you are affected by them is vital. If the Chakras are in proper alignment many ailments can be overcome or effectively managed.

Crystals are believed to have the ability to align body vibrations and release the Chakras life force energies in order to unblock them and restore their balance.

Practitioners of crystal healing place stones on areas of their client's bodies to balance the chakras. The technique of placing crystals on the body promotes healing known as 'laying on of stones'.

It is believed to be one of the most powerful techniques for cleansing negative energy and balancing the chakras.

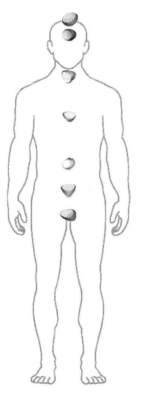

7. Crown Chakra
6. Third eye Chakra

5. Throat Chakra

4. Heart Chakra

3. Solar plexus Chakra
2. Navel Chakra
1. Root Chakra

Specially prepared crystals are used to align the body's vibration with the planet, in the process freeing the life force energy in the chakras to transform negative energy into positive energy. A common layout used by crystal healing practitioners is to place a single crystal on the body at the location corresponding to each chakra. Use either clear quartz or the color associated with that particular chakra.

A selection of suitable crystals for placement on each Chakra is shown in the following table.

CHAKRA	CRYSTAL
First Or Root Chakra	Garnet , Red Jasper, Ruby
Second Or Navel Chakra	Carnelian, Fire Opal, Orange Calcite
Third Or Solar Plexus Chakra	Citrine, Honey Calcite, Yellow Jasper
Fourth Or Heart Chakra	Emerald, Green Aventurine, Malachite
Fifth Or Throat Chakra	Aquamarine, Blue Agate, Turquoise
Sixth Or Third Eye Chakra	Lapis Lazuli, Sodalite, Sapphire
Seventh Or Crown Chakra	Amethyst, Clear Quartz

HOW TO CHOOSE CRYSTALS

Crystals are available in many forms with varying purposes and not all types of crystals, or even crystals of the same type, will have the same results or work in the same way for different individuals.

Since we are all unique, we will experience crystals in different ways and you have to make sure you choose the right one for you.

As a starting point, make sure that you have clearly identified what you want a crystal to achieve. Your next course of action should be to consult a crystal healing practitioner to identify some crystal varieties with properties that match your desired outcome.

When choosing a specific crystal specimen the most important thing is to determine whether it has a good vibrational match for your purpose. Selecting a crystal that will raise and not lower your vibrational frequency is, thus, of critical importance.

An experienced user of crystals can 'feel' if a crystal is right for them by just holding it. At first you may finds this difficult, but as you become more attuned to your body and senses it will become crystal clear as to which crystal is right for you.

State your purpose in terms of what you want to do, not what you want to stop doing. You should find that your feelings change when holding or visualizing different crystals and stating your purpose. Some will appear to have no effect. Some may even make you feel a little flat or sad.

Crystals that are in tune with your vibrational frequency and purpose should give you a lift in mind, body, and spirit. You may feel uplifted, have an overall sense of happiness, find yourself full of energy, or you might recall happy memories that bring a beaming smile to your face.

POPULAR CRYSTALS AND THEIR PROPERTIES

There are a great many crystals that can be used for a multitude of purposes and in time you will find the ones that work best for you.

As a starting point, here are some popular crystals with a brief description of their properties and uses.

ALABASTER

Used to assist meditation.

AMBER

Used to help in healing of allergies, arthritis and back pain. Believed to oxygenate and strengthen the blood stream.

AMETHYST

Used to ease migraines and headaches and to oxygenate and strengthen the blood.

APATITE

Used to help curb appetite and to oxygenate and strengthen the blood stream.

BLOODSTONE (HELIOTROPE, CHALCEDONY)

Used to oxygenate and strengthen the blood stream.

CALCITE

Used to aid the kidneys, pancreas and spleen.

CITRINE

Used to aid the digestive organs and heart.

COLBALTOCALCITE

Used to increase harmony and release buried emotions.

CORAL

Used to stimulate the blood stream and remove impurities from the blood.

DIAMOND

Used to dispel negativity and enhance brain function.

EMERALD

Used to enhance memory, improve focus and aid harmony.

FLUORITE

Used to aid concentration and strength teeth and bones.

FULGURITES

Used to recharge physical and mental energy.

HEMATITE

Used to increase resistance to stress and help to circulate oxygen throughout the body.

IOLITE

Used to expand spiritual vision and bring harmony.

JADE

Used to attract wealth, prosperity and love.

KYANITE

Used to increase insight and enhance psychic abilities.

LAPIS LAZULI

Used to release tension and increase strength, vitality and virility.

LEPIDOLITE

Used to aid sleep and help with emotional and mental balance and stability.

MALACHITE

Used to help with the release of fear and resolve inner tensions.

MOONSTONE

Used to promote harmony and good fortune in marriages and relationships.

OBSIDIAN

Used to dispel negativity and provide wisdom and love.

OPAL

Used to aid eyesight and enhance intuition.

PIETERSITE

Used to enhance strength, courage and willpower.

ROSE QUARTZ

Used to clear resentment, fear, guilt and jealousy.

RUBY

Used to strengthen immunity, courage and integrity.

SAPPHIRE

Used to stimulate psychic abilities, inspiration, loyalty and love.

SERPENTINE

Used to promote calmness and balanced emotions.

SODALITE

Used to calm the mind and bring clarity and truth.

TANZANITE

Used to increase fertility and enhance psychic abilities.

TIGER EYE

Used to enhance perception and insight.

TOPAZ

Used to strengthen many internal organs and aid in the cure of many ailments.

TOURMALINE

Used to aid concentration and enhance sensitivity, inspiration and understanding.

TURQUOISE

Used to aid emotional balance and promote creative expression.

VIVIANITE

Used to remove negative energy and provide peace and calm.

WAVELLITE

Used to help with emotional healing and meditation.

YELLOW JASPER

Used to give protection from negativity and depression.

FINAL WORDS

Crystals have amazing properties; you only have to accept the abilities the crystals possess to harness their power to improve your life.

If you decide to experiment with crystals yourself, decide what you want to achieve and make sure you choose a crystal that matches your desired outcome and is in tune with your vibrational energy.

Remember to cleanse and energize the crystal before you use it and make sure you cleanse and re-energize it regularly.

I hope you have enjoyed reading this book and that it has given you information that you will find helpful in the future.

If you would like to know more about natural healing therapies, you may be interested in my other books which are also available on Amazon:

Aromatherapy and Essential Oils Explained

The Basics of Chakra Healing in 30 Minutes or Less

Chakra Balancing for Beginners

Learn Reiki Healing in 30 Minutes or Less

Natural Remedies

Beginner's Zen

An Introduction to Meditation

In closing I would like to thank you again for choosing this book and I wish you good health and good fortune for the future.

LEGAL DISCLAIMER

While the information in this book is presented in good faith and every care has been taken to ensure that the information contained herein is accurately presented, individual results will vary and the author does not guarantee the outcome of using any information or technique contained in this book.

The information provided in this book is designed to provide helpful information on the subjects discussed. This book is not meant to be used, nor should it be used, to diagnose or treat any medical condition. For diagnosis or treatment of any medical problem, you should consult your own physician.

The publisher and author are not responsible for any specific health or allergy needs that may require medical supervision and are not liable for any damages or negative consequences from any treatment, action, application or preparation, to any person reading or following the information in this book.

You should always seek appropriate professional advice before commencing any course of action based on the information contained in this book.

ABOUT THE AUTHOR

Lindsey James has a passionate interest in natural therapies for health and wellbeing. She is currently working on a series of books to introduce the benefits of natural alternative therapies to a wider audience.

Printed in Great Britain
by Amazon

72640910R00020